Scotland
THE TEXT

Scotland
THE TEXT

You Can Take My Phone,
But You'll Never Take My Freedom

ERIN DUFFY

BLACK & WHITE PUBLISHING

First published 2016
by Black & White Publishing Ltd
29 Ocean Drive, Edinburgh EH6 6JL

1 3 5 7 9 10 8 6 4 2   16 17 18 19

ISBN: 978 1 78530 063 9

Design and arrangement © Black & White Publishing 2016

A CIP catalogue record for this book is available from the British Library.

Contents

Robert
BURNS

Renowned Poet and Scotland's own Casanova, 1759–1796

You wanna come over? Just finished writing something, I want to see if you think it's any good.

Sure, I'll head over in five minutes.

No wait, scratch that. Mary's just got here ;)
*Anna
**Elizabeth
*** Jenny
********JEAN. I meant Jean...

Oh no. Ohhhh no no no no.

What's wrong?!

I am a terrible person.

What happened!!

I have broken Nature's social union.

I am none the wiser.

The poor wee beastie! Why must I be haunted by both past and future?

Uhhh. What?

I RAN OVER A MOUSE'S NEST WITH THE PLOUGH

Ohhhh. That is quite bad. It's ok, he can build another one?

IT'S WINTER, GARY!

Mary,
QUEEN OF SCOTS

Queen of Scotland and a generally unlucky lady, 1542–1587

Hey cousin Liz, guess who's coming to visit!

Oh hey . . . umm you?

Surprise! I just really needed to get away.

How long are you staying for?

Not sure, just until this whole thing with the nobles blows over. They keep killing my husbands and locking me in castles and stuff, it's really pissing me off.

Omg come to England! That sounds awful!

I know right. FML

Did you want to come for dinner this weekend? This castle is lovely, much nicer than the last one you put me up in. Lonely though! It would be nice to see you.

Can't this weekend.

That's a shame! What are you up to?

Washing my hair.

Woaaaah! Ok another time!

Liz, thanks so much for letting me stay so long but I'm thinking I'd quite like to go back to Scotland now. It has been 19 years . . .

Liz?

Hellooo?

. . . .

WHY DOES THIS KEEP HAPPENING TO ME

Alexander
GRAHAM BELL

Inventor of the ringing communication device, 1847–1922

Ring ring

Ring ring

What?

Ring ring

You're doing this wrong

What

Ring ring ring ring

You shouldn't answer the phone like that It's rude

But we're not on the phone!

Ring ring

Ring ring

Say words

Call me

Why?

Call me

Call me call me call me

Call me

WHY DO I HAVE TO CALL YOU WHEN WE'RE TEXTING RIGHT NOW?

BECAUSE I INVENTED TELEPHONES FOR A REASON SO JUST CALL ME

Ring ring

You know Mike, I'm almost sad about telephones becoming a thing

Man, don't say that! What's got you down bro?

It's just this girl ✶

Oh boy. Continue . . . ?

Well
She keeps calling me.
And I really like her . . .

Bro that's great!
What's the problem?

It's just...
I know when that hotline bling
That can only mean one thing

. . . That she's dialled your number?
Sorry man, I'm confused?

I threw a wish in the well

What? Who's this?

Don't ask me I'll never tell.

Alex, is that you?

Pennies and dimes for a kiss

I know it's you, Alex. Stop being such a perv.

Ripped jeans

Skin was showing

Are you watching me?

You creep!

Where are you?

Hot night

Wind was blowing

What are you doing outside??

Goodbye Alex.

Where you think you're going baby?

OMG IS THAT YOU IN
THE BUSHES!??

Hey I just met you

And this is crazy

YEA NO SHIT!

But here's my number

So call me maybe!

I object to this book.

. . .

Anyone else?

No?

Fine!

🙁

William
WALLACE

Badass Scottish warrior during the Wars of Scottish Independence, 1270–1305

Ok, you guys join the attack in five mins

Now!!!

Where have you gone?

WHERE'S THE CAVALRY

We weren't feeling very well . . .

I don't care if you don't feel well, Duncan's lost an arm and he's still here!

The whole bloody lot of ye have disappeared, come back now!

I just asked and no one's keen.

Too many English.

But we're losing!!

Mmm. Did you do that thing where you show them your bums yet?

Yes, it didn't work this time – COME BACK!

FREEEEDOOMMMMM

Eugh

What is it now, William?

Just wanted to remind you

Of what?

That hundreds of years from now my heroic struggles and the blood of my men will be used as the basis of a terrible movie that will make a mockery of me and my people.

Oh . . .

Well, that sucks

A MOCKERY.

You have to help me!

What's up Will??

A crazy man is planning to torture me and punish the whole of Scotland!

Oh no!

Has king Edward captured you?

Yes yes, never mind that!

But he'll hang, draw and quarter you!

This is awful!

Yea it sucks but listen . . .

Apparently Mel Gibson wants to make a film about my life and the Scottish fight for independence!

You have to stop him!

OMG we're all doomed!

Bonnie
PRINCE CHARLIE

Scotland's foremost romantic lead and Battler of the English, 1720–1788

> Charles, it really is now or never. We've got to get you out of here before the English arrive!

I'm not coming.

> Why not?! Are you hurt?

I have NOTHING to wear.

It's embarrassing.

> Wow

White or blue blouse? I don't want to draw too much attention.

> You don't want to draw ANY attention!

So blue then

????

Help meeeee

> I'm trying! You have to leave for Skye now!

So do I need sensible shoes?

> We have clothes for you here

> We've got to disguise you as a woman

> Please hurry, the English are not far off.

Are you sure it's not the fashion police . . .

David
LIVINGSTONE

Went on lots of holidays to Africa, 1813–1873

> David, how are you getting on? Haven't heard from you in a while!

Terribly. I'm completely lost. Not even sure what the Heart of Africa looks like tbh.

> Ahh sorry to hear that! Have you tried Google Maps?

Nah, they haven't invented it yet.

> Oh right. Well shall we send someone to try and find you?

Yeah I think that's best. I'm not feeling too good.

> Ok will do. They should be with you in about 7–8 months!

Brilliant.

Robert
LOUIS STEVENSON

Wrote some great books, you'll know them when you hear the titles,
1850–1894

Hey Rob

Yes?

Why can't you play
cards on a pirate ship?

Cause the captain keeps
standing on the deck!

Hmm, good one.

Very amusing.

I WROTE THIS AMAZING NOVELLA DO U WANT TO READ IT?

God man, calm down!

IT'S SO FREAKING GOOD

Hahaha I'm sure it is pal

IT'S ABOUT THIS DOCTOR AND THIS OTHER DUDE

BUT

WAIT FOR IT . . .

THEY'RE THE SAME PERSON!

Ooh interesting! Yeah I'll give it a read ✪

. . . Too late, I burnt it

Why?!

It's all part of The Process

Ffs Louis

Congrats, Robert!

Jekyll and Hyde is selling like hot cross buns!

Fab!

(does anyone like hot cross buns?)

I suppose I should leave the similes to you, Robert . . .

Anyway, I was thinking you should write another gothic set in London.

It's topical, it's similar – it's perfect!

Um OK, maybe . . .

How many copies has Jekyll and Hyde sold, exactly?

It's sold over 40 000 copies!

Just imagine how many the Ripper book will sell!

Can you give that figure to me in Pina Coladas?

What?

How many Pina Coladas does 40 000 copies translate into?

Robert, no!

Yes!

No! Don't you dare!

We can go to the tropics

Sip Pina Coladas

Shorty I could take you there!

Robert! You're staying here in Britain and writing a Gothic!

Do I make myself clear?

If you like Pina Coladas, and NOT getting caught in the rain . . .

Robert!

See you on Treasure Island!

Burke
AND Hare

Robbed many a grave and great lovers of skeletons, active 1828

Burke

Yes?

Margaret says we've got a new tenant

I'll grab the whisky
Oh, and the tea chest

Nah I think we're gonna need something a tad bigger for this heffer

Herring barrel?

Aye

I'll see you at the lodge

Burke

Yes?

Nothing

Well it's just that the missus
has been saying things
about Helen Helen

My Helen?

Yes Helen

Well Mrs Hare don't think we
can trust since you know

No.

Well since she's Scotch

No.

No what

We're not killing her
and that's final.

It's always been my dream to start a B&B . . .

Do you want to start one with me, Burke?

I'm not sure, Hare . . .

I always wanted to have a butchers shop, tbh.

Hmm . . .

I think we can sort something out.

Damn it Hare, we've got a competitor!

Someone else is selling corpses to the university?

No, someone else just opened a B&B . . .

Sawney
BEAN

Eater of many a human hamburger, somewhere between the 13th and 16th centuries

What's for tea the night?

You

Lol

Jk

I'll pick someone up on my way home

OK

Cheers bae

Robert
THE Bruce

Warrior for Independence and general spider admirer, 1274–1329

Yer free now

Whit?

I said YER FREE NOW

You know, cause I beat the English

Yer welcome.

Oh aye

Thanks Bruce

Don't you just love spiders?

No really Bruce

Bonnie wee things, aren't they?

Just braw what they can do.

Tenacious wee buggers too!

Edward?

Yes?

Give it a rest would ye?

No.

Remember Bannockburn?

Yes.

And Loudoun Hill?

Well?

Yes.

I remember.

Well, don't ye think
its time to give up?

No.

Rob?

What?

You know I told you Scotland was going to have an independence referendum?

Yes! Did it work?

Umm

No.

Damn it!!!

. . .

But we still have an alliance with France, right?

. . .

Bruce, I need to tell you about something called 'Brexit'

Alexander
FLEMING

Discoverer of penicillin (thanks, friend), 1881–1955

Where are my samples?

Oh hello Mr Fleming. What samples

The ones on my desk.

The ones that were labelled 'samples'.

Well I don't know anything about no samples Mr Fleming

The petri dishes?

Small round glass dishes.

With bacteria growing in the jelly.

Oh those! I thought they'd gone mouldy so I chucked them in the bin

You threw away my samples?

I guess I did

Sorry about that sir. It's just not very hygienic, I thought

Well you were quite mistaken.

In the future I'd appreciate it if you left my work be and busied yourself elsewhere.

John
LOGIE Baird

Pioneer of the television (the forerunner of Netflix), 1888–1946

> Two hundred channels and nothing on.

> Are you complaining to me?

> No.

> Just making an observation.

Darling, what is the big box in the sitting room?

Press the big button on the front

JESUS H CHRIST

Darling, come quick

Come home plz

There are people in there

It's ok, it's a recording! I invented it!

I don't know what you're talking about

We have to help this man

Why is he so small

Can he see me?

JOHN I AM IN MY DRESSING GOWN

David
HUME

Philosopher, historian, essayist, economist and all round smart chap,
1711–1776

Reason is, and ought only to be
the slave of the passions, and can
never pretend to any other office
than to serve and obey them.

Eh?

Come again

He is happy whom circumstances
suit his temper; but he is more
excellent who suits his temper to
any circumstance.

Dave no one knows
what yer on about.

Beauty in things exists
in the mind which
contemplates them.

See this is why yer
not married

I know ☆

I do believe that one day people will erect giant, beautiful buildings in my name

Oh yeah . . .

Seems a bit UNREASONABLE

And they will adorn my statue with many gifts

Prized possessions, culture's tokens of gratitude and respect

They will kneel at my golden feet, and seek enlightenment

Mmm. Guess we'll never know

James
WATT

Inventor of the first choo-choo puff-puff, 1736–1819

Hey Jimmy

Hi

It's James btw

You still playing with trains?

Yes. I like trains.

And boiling water?

Yes. Steam engines are very effective.

Aye for making tea

James

Yep

This new steam train idea

Yep

Call me a moron, but I still don't get it

We've been through this.

I know, but Layman's terms

Big, powerful, mechanical vehicle, shaped like a long metal cylinder on wheels, has a steam engine and goes really fast and transports things around

I'm still none the wiser

I don't know how else to describe it!

I know, but I just can't seeee it

Can't you just trust me and invest in it?

Explain it in horses

What?

Horses. How many horses.

You want me to compare a machine with the power of horses.

Yeah, like one train = how many horses. 10?

You might actually be onto something . . .

SIR Walter SCOTT

He wrote *Waverley*, and enjoyed having stuff named after him and his novels, 1771–1832

> So have you had a chance to look at Waverley yet?

> I don't know Walt.

> You must remember that prose fiction is aesthetically inferior to poetry.

> Am I right in saying it's not even a tragedy?

> Well no, I suppose it's not

> It'll never sell, Walt.

If thou would'st view fair Melrose aright,
Go visit it by the pale moonlight.

Why would I ever go
to Melrose?

O Caledonia! stern and wild,
Meet nurse for a poetic child!
Land of brown heath and shaggy wood;
Land of the mountain and the flood!

You know it's like a
snooker table in Tiree.

SIR Arthur CONAN DOYLE

Sherlock, Sherlock, Sherlock, 1859–1930

So I was thinking about this writing a new book

Another Sherlock Holmes adventure?

No

Actually I was thinking about writing some science fiction

??

Sorry

Are you being serious?

No I'm being absolutely genuine

It's about a hidden plateau in the Amazon basin in South America where scientists discover prehistoric animals!

Dinosaurs?

Your new book is about dinosaurs?

Well yes

I'd stick to Holmes if I were you

It's out Tuesday

Hey, I've been thinking . . .

My Sherlock Holmes series needs a new direction, be braver, more 'out there'.

Arthur, it's great as it is.

But it could be better!

Remember the dinosaurs?

Yes . . .

'Sir Conan Doyle's new novel is clearly a work of self-discovery – it features the revelation of prehistoric dinosaurs from another time and place. Doyle appears to be in a similar state of isolation from his readers and their sensibilities. We want good old Sherlock Holmes!'

The *Daily Telegraph* people are a bunch of conservatives . . .

'Utter horse manure.'

Yes yes, but the *Daily Mail* doesn't like me anyway. Just listen to my idea:

Sherlock Holmes lives in a futuristic London – let's say the early twenty first century – and solves crimes like he does now, but with the aid of technology!

And I'll write it as a script for theatre, and we'll find a handsome young man with dark curls to play the title role!

And we'll need a snappier title, like *Holmes*, or *Sherlock*!

It sounds stupid. Can you imagine what the papers will say?

Ah well, maybe you're right.

Let's leave it . . .

Arthur?

Um

Yes, Mr Bell?

This Holmes fellow you're writing about

Yes?

Does he remind you of anyone in particular?

Well

I suppose I may have slightly based him on you

Just a teensy little bit

That makes me a bit uncomfortable

Why?

It's just cause I like you so much

I can see that

Why doesn't he like women?

No reason

K

You killed Holmes

Um

Yes

Who is this?

WHY

I wanted to work on
more serious writing.

Seriously though
who are you?

How did you get
this number?

BRING HIM BACK!

. . .

Um no?

Maggie
DICKSON

She may have been hanged, but no one can hold this lady down,
1702(ish)–1765(ish)

Knock knock

Who's there

Me

Me who?

Me

Maggie in the coffin

STILL ALIVE BTW

John?

John are you there?

I didn't want to do this over the phone

Well I can't come to work anymore

I'm pregnant and it's your baby

It's okay though, I'm gonna take care of it you know

So just don't worry about me

Call me pls!

King
JAMES I/VI

Top King of Great Britain, 1566–1625

> Help pls!

> I'm having a bit of an identity crisis

> !!!

>> Yeah

>> What's up?

> Well

> I'm having issues with the whole being two different people thing

>> What do you mean two different people?

> Well how can I be James the first and the sixth?

>> That does sound like an issue :/

>> Have you talked to your parents about it?

> No

> They're dead.

>> You really do have issues Jim

> WHO IS JIM?

>> You must be the wisest fool in Christendom

Hey, u ever seen Game of Thrones?

Duh, who hasn't

I think it's written about me

Uhh

Sorry what

Yup. I think I'm the heir to the Iron Throne

Just think about it.

Lord
MACBETH

Scottish Military Leader (fun fact: he was a real guy), popularised in 1611 by Shakespeare as being a bit of a girl's blouse, 1005–1057

So

Did you really kill Duncan?

Nay

My men killed Duncan

But he was such a good king!

No.

He was young, weak and ineffective

Are you sure?

Yes.

You're thinking of the play, birthed from nonsense

What about the witches?

NO I say!

Well

Yeah?

Actually there was one . . .

Hey babe, need 2 talk 2 u xo

What is it, Macbeth?

Babe dnt be mad xo

But I was talking 2 these 3 witches rite

. . . Where are you going with this?

Well. They said I'd b King of Scotland rite

And I dunno wot 2 think???

King of Scotland??

Yh babe xo

. . . I'd be Queen of Scotland, then?

I guess so babe xoxo

Sweetie we should probably invite Duncan round for dinner soon xx

OK but y? xo

No reason, my darling. Come home quickly <3

Hey MacBeth . . .

Hey MacDuff!

I've been trying to get hold of my wife and kids but they're not replying . . .

Oh?

Yea, just wondering if something's up?

No, they're good.

OK great! Was getting worried.

I'll try them again later.

☺ (y) *

Saint
NINIAN

All round nice guy, somewhere in the 4th–5th centuries

> Was your father really a Christian king?

> ??

> Did you really meet Saint Martin?

> What about performing miracles?

> Is that true?

> Is any of it true?

> Hello?

> Ninian?

> I'm afraid that there is no unchallenged historical evidence to support any of these stories.

CHARLES Rennie MACKINTOSH

A celebrated artist with some serious style, 1868–1928

The light

It is majestic

You okay?

It is so holistic

Pouring in from the east

Yeah

And does it not evoke a calming and organic feeling to the interior?

Who's interior?

The room's!

Oh

You're talking about that chair aren't you

Of course I am!

Such simple and elegant design!

Such beautiful and long geometric shapes <3

Is it comfy?

What do you mean?

Is it comfortable to sit in?

. . .

Why does that matter?

going 2 be late

oh for goodness sake

where are you

strugglng

completely tangled up in my necktie

legs and all

I always told you it was too flouncy

I'm an ARTIST

Lord
KELVIN

Did good science, 1824–1907

Is it warm outside today?

Yeah

I suppose

I'd still wear long sleeves though

How warm would you say it is?

Dunno

Maybe twenty degrees?

Don't be ridiculous!

That's FREEZING

No it's not

It's like room temp

No

Room temp is about 200 degrees

You know nothing about thermodynamics

...

did you start this conversation just to do that?

Yes

Did you feel the burn?

At how many degrees would I have to feel it?

...

no one uses Kelvin

You and the missus want to come for dinner?

I can't I'm half way across the sodding Atlantic

Sorry I asked

Do you have ANY IDEA how difficult it is to lay underwater cables

errrrm

no I can't say I do

Well I bloody do

. . .

It is SO HARD

George
CLEGHORN

Discoverer of the noble gin and tonic, 1716–1794

George?

Yes?

We've decided to reassign you to Dublin

No

What?

Sorry can't do it

What do you mean you can't do it?

I just need to

To finish my research here

You know, in the Med.

I'll send word when I'm done

Kk bye!

I've done it!

Done what?

I've found a cure for Malaria!

For what

The disease?

Malaria?

The one all our troops keep dying of?

Oh yeah

What about it?

I've got a cure!

Yeah

What's that

Quinine bark dissolved in water

That sounds disgusting

Actually, the tonic water goes rather well with gin

iu the rsjhuss iss fjueel

I m relaay hdrunk

Cous girn is soo deliciius

Sandford
FLEMING

Inventor of a slightly confusing way to tell the time,
which somehow became 'standard', 1827–1915

What time's your train?

6:45

OK

I'll pick you up before work then

No

6:45 in the evening

PM

That'll be 18:45 then

There's no 18 o'clock

Kirkpatrick
MACMILLAN

Inventor of the glorious two wheeled bicycle, 1812–1878

Macmillan?

Yes?

You're pedal bike design has made me tons of cash

That's nice

Pity you didn't even patent your own idea

Eh?

Not really

What do you mean?

Well Gavin

I'm not really too bothered either way

I just like to cycle

And my bike made it easy

So you don't want the money?

Nah

Moneys no an issue with me

I just spent five shillings compensating a little girl I knocked down on my way to Glasgow

I've got heaps of money

But people are saying you didn't actually invennnnt it

You can tell me

Tell me tell me tell me

I DID invent it

Did you?!

I did

I wheely wheely did

;)

This is not a laughing matter.

Alexander
SELKIRK

The real Robinson Crusoe, 1676–1721

> Helloooooooo

> Anyone?

> PLS send help

> So lonely!!!!!

Guuuyyyyz help meee

I'm getting rly bored

There's nothing to do heeeere

If this was a book it'd suck

Hello, Mr. Selkirk.

Hey, who's this?

It's Daniel Defoe.

I'm writing a book based on your shipwreck. Can you tell me about any of the adventures you had?

Adventures?

Didn't really have any.

Oh I'm sure you had loads! What did you do there for 24 years?

You mean 4 years?

Right . . .

Not much . . .

Built a hut.

Ate some goats.

Fished.

No fierce animals?

Not really.

There were some rats, but I tamed a cat.

A panther, perhaps??

Just a little tomcat.

I see . . .

What about savages?

There was no one else there.

Ah ok . . .

Mr. Selkirk, what is your stance on artistic license?

Oh I don't mind it . . .

Good!

So long as you don't make anything up and I'm allowed to proof read and veto.

Hello?

Hello?

Mr. Defoe?

Deacon
WILLIAM BRODIE

A pillar of the community, known gambler, mistress-keeper, robber of houses and father to a brood of illegitimate bairns. Possibly the original lad, 1741–1788

Dad

Hello

Heloooooooo

We know you're there

We?

Yeah

We

How many kids did you think you had?

I think I have some calls to make

bye

Want to know the definition of irony

What?

They're going to hang me with the gallows I designed

That's not irony

Do you even know what irony is

It's just coincidence

Like I didn't feel bad enough

Soz bro

Good luck for tmro!

Captain
KIDD

A real life pirate! 1645–1701

I just like ships, that's all

And maybe gold too, I guess

Is that such a crime?

Bro u cnt go round taking other pplz ships

its not vry friendly

But everyone loves a cheeky plunder now and again!

And it was just a wee one

. . . A few times

Not kl, man

not kl

You stole my ship!

soz!

. . . and sank it!

oops . . .

And you *killed* all my men!

It's ok – I was just Kidding!

. . .

Seriously tho it's what I do.

William
TOPAZ McGONAGALL

A really bad poet, 1825–1902

Glorious friend, fellow citizen of Dundee!
Long has our communication been
unattendee (-d)

Wot do u want Willie

Ah nothing but some companionable chatter,
. . . Although I'll admit, dearest friend,
I'm getting no fatter

Aye? Tht so?

Life as a poet is but a poor existence,
The purse strings of my readers gives me
awful resistance

U wnting a loan again Willie?

Well since you mentioned it . . .

Aye

Hi, I'm getting in touch from the Writers Workshop that your wife recommended? Our classes are Tuesdays and Thursdays at 6pm.

Whit you sayin

Sorry, no – she just mentioned you might like to come and told me to get in touch.

Ahm a world class poet, lady

Fed up with this stuff fae people who don't understand literature

Sorry to cause offence. It wasn't intended! Your wife simply said you had received some bad feedback, so asked if I could help.

Bad feedback! Aye I get shouted at in thi street!

Don't need it fae you too!

I don't even knw you

Sorry to hear that. Never mind.

Haters gon' hate

Charles MacKINTOSH

Made waterproofs a reality, 1766–1843

Sup wifey

I got u a present ;)

> yh? is it a surprise? ;D

yh ul nvr guess wot it is

coz I jst invented it ;)

> babe u r sooooo talented!!

> Cnt w8 til ur home ;)

Same bbz

il giv u a clue

ul nvr hav 2 be wet again :P

> ...?!?!?!?!

John
MUIR

Liked being outside, 1838–1914

Good morning, rocks ✪

Good morning, trees ✪

I find your silence comforting

No one understands me like you do

Good morning, blue sky ✪

Your painted clouds, so sublime and awesome

Good morning, small bunny rabbit ✪

Hello, sun. My oldest friend

Are you coming back for breakfast?

Stop oppressing me, woman!

SIR Robert
A WATSON-WATT

Developer of radar (Tinder for aeroplanes), 1892–1973

Hey grl ;)

Hi

U must be a Messerschmitt Bf 109 ;)

. . . I'm a wot?

Coz ur coming up on my radar ;)

. . .

Nd ur da bomb xoxo

Yh bye

You'll never guess what just happened

What . . .

I just got a speeding ticket

Oh poop

It gets worse. What do you think the policeman used?

ONLY A BLOODY RADAR GUN

Well at least you know your invention works?

Would never have made it if I knew I'd be getting this sort of treatment. Don't they know who I am?

Lady
MACBETH

Character in Shakespeare's *MacBeth*, who didn't take any nonsense,
play first performed 1611

Well . . . ?

Yes dear?

Is he dead yet?

Yes dear

And the daggers are planted?

Eh, no dear, not yet

What do you mean, 'not yet'??

Eh . . . I'm a wee bit shaken my love

What with all the murder etc

MacBeth get back in there or yir no getting any for a month

But baaaaabe

Ffs I'm getting sick of cleaning up after you

Greyfriars
BOBBY

The most loyal pup known to man, 19th century

John?

Jooooooohn?

John I'm hungry

John this isn't funny anymore

Right I'll wait but I'm no amused

People think I'm guarding your grave

But really I'm just sitting here looking sad

So then people feed me LOL

#lifehacks

Hey Bobby, why u so down?

It's this guy . . .

He's stealing my trick.

Your trick?

I stand at John's grave all day and people feel sorry for me and feed me.

What's this guy doing?

He's standing outside the cemetery on a bloody pedestal.

People are flocking around him . . .

And he Never. Ever. Takes. A. Break . . .

Dude that's a statue of you . . .

I think I'm in love!

Who with, Bobby?

This lassie I saw.

Which lassie?

The lassie on TV.

You mean *the* Lassie?

Yea! We'd be like the Brangelina of the dog celeb world!

More like Michael Douglas and Catherine Zeta Jones

You are way too old for her!

She's not that young, must be at least 60 now!

Yea, and you're like 160!

MISS Jean BRODIE

A fictional character from Muriel Spark's *The Prime of Miss Jean Brodie*, published 1961. A woman in her prime, as she likes to remind the reader.

Sandy dear, who would you rank as the top five most handsome gentlemen in Edinburgh?

am I no a bit young for this?

Not at all

A woman needs to know what she wants, so she can plan her future

And planning is essential, if you are to make the most of your prime

if u say so, miss

You never know when your prime is just around the corner

I was lucky

I knew when my prime began

And I have many years left in my prime

ffs away wi yir prime ya baggage

yir past yir sell by date, face it

. . . an' yir maw, fur aw 5

;)

Tam
O'SHANTER

Protagonist in Robert Burns' poem of the same name, published 1790.
A cheeky scamp who spied on the wrong party.

wr r u??

Tam if ur no hame in 10 mins thur's nae supper

Nane o that, wr r u??

bae I lv u

BABE ur so beautiful

n stuff lv u bao.

. . . bt I broke horse

U WOT?

thr ws this church rite

n this burd rite

SO FIT

XCUSE ME?

I mean, lk, athletic eh

no lyk

. . . fit fit.

anyway aye

the horse is ok lyk

Tailless tho

Awright bbe ;) saw u oot the nite

Who is this?

Bbe I'll be everything u want a man 2 b ;)

Is this the man from the Church . . . ?

So uv been thinkin aboot me then ;)

The man who was peering through the windows and catcalling me . . . ?

Jst appreciating the show bbe ;)

Please don't contact me again.

Rob Roy
MacGREGOR

The Robin Hood of the North, 1671–1735

Now Rob if you'd just be reasonable . . .

REASONABLE?! Dinnae gie me yir reason laddie!!

But I need ur rent Rob, soz pal!

Dinnae you be callin pul, PAL. G'on an bile yir heid!!!

Rob

look I'm rly sorry

but it's nae rent = nae house 😞

F9

it's nae hoose then, ya thieving bam

but this is WAR oan u an yir clan!!

>:(

J.M. BARRIE

Creator of Peter Pan and sporter of an excellent moustache, 1860–1937

> But muuuuum I jst want to write!

> Enuff James, a man's gotta go out and earn a living xxxx

> No mum, I don't wanna!! U can't make me!!

> I h8 u

> Now now, son. U'll thank me one day xxxx

> Nuht

> I'm gonna run away

> I nvr wanna grow up!

> Don't be ridiculous James xxxx

Fancy a wee spot of cricket tomorrow?

Ok old chap. Although I'm not terribly good.

Love a good dress up though! I'll be there

Who else is involved?

Just a few pals. Pretty informal

Grand. Anyone I know?

A.A. Milne?

Goodness gracious. Well, I've certainly heard of him!

H.G. Wells

Him too. Rather intimidating!

Rudyard Kipling

Arthur Conan Doyle

Walter Raleigh

😑

Errrm Jerome K. Jerome

PG Wodehouse

George Bernard Shaw might pop along

Yes right not sure I can make it actually.

Hugh MacDIARMID

Primarily an excellent poet and a big thistle fan, 1892–1978

Hv u ever thot about how gr8 thistles r?

Not really

U know wot this country needs?

What does this country need, Hugh?

Moar thistles

Thistles r everything

Are you drunk, pal

Nooooope

Writing some poetry

Looking at some thislses

Thislets

Thsletis

Alright, don't hurt yersel

Well I am hurt. Inside

Look at this country

It's ok Hugh. Everything's ok.

But LIFE

So fleeting

What is temporality?

Oh Scotland

D'ye ever think about what it must be like to live under the sea

I honestly don't know what to do with this

DR Jekyll & MR Hyde

Our protagonists (protagonist?) from Robert Louis Stevenson's novel of the same name, published 1886. Just goes to show what one drink can do to a fellow.

Go on, jst a wee one ;)

> Go away.

C'mon lad, wots lyf wivout a cheeky murder now n then

> I said GO AWAY

It'll be top banter tho

get on the bevvy, cheeky murder aftr a few

> I h8 u

B4 u no it we'll be on the lash in banter city

Having sum laughs

maybe beat sum folks 2 death

> Y r u still here

I am the banter king

Kneel b4 me

DRINK IIIITTT

No

Drink it drink it drink it drink it drink it

G'waaaaan drink it

NO

I'll just wait until you're asleep and then I'll come out anyway

Drink it!!!

Oh my god FINE

ffs

This really can't continue though

brb

hey

hey

oooh this is fun

texting myself!

So how come your name is Hyde?

Because I'm within your "hyde"

lol

I'm a side of yourself that you "hyde"

Haha!

"Ye kylling" me XD

That's trying too hard, Jekyll.

☺

☹

Connor
MACLEOD

There can only be one.
Original TV series 'Highlander' launched 1992

Knock knock

Who's there?

Immortality

Och Connor no again

Aye but . . .

It never gits auld

Hahahahahananaaha

Yir the wurst

Dolly
THE Sheep

The first mammal to be cloned for Roslin's growing clone sheep army, 1996–2003 (look to the Internet for the fun science behind our woolly friend).

Baaaaah

> Dolly what is it?

BAAAAH!

> Dolly if you have the capacity to understand and make use of written communication then you have the capacity to communicate verbally too

Baaaaah.

> Right be like that

Idiot

I may be a clone, but I'm still a sheep

> SEE?!

I mean . . .

baaaaaaah

Adam
SMITH

A man all about the Enlightenment, 1723–1790

Hey friend, wanna come round 4 dinner?

Yh maybe. I mite be free, wot r u making?

Havnt thought about it yet

BUT I'm writin this new book and I'd luv 2 talk about it wiv some1

U know, get some outside opinions

Aww that's nice Adam, what's it about?

Lots of stuff

Like economics n stuff. Theres like 5 books in the 1 book so theres lots 2 discuss

That sounds gr8, Adam

Gd luk with it

Bt am rly soz I jst remembered ive got 2 wash my aunt's cat

O ok

Say hi 2 Mr Tiddlesworth 4 me

John
KNOX

Big fan of the Protestant Church, not a fan of Mary, QoS, 1505–1572

Wot do u call a sleepwalking nun?

giv it a rest man

A roamin' Catholic!!!

could've been worse I guess . . .

I hav moar

Maybe save them 4 another time?

F9 I'll go tell them 2 bae

That's if I can find her amid her sea of royal cats

Wot?

U know Mary, she's a real Cat-holic

Yeh maybe dont lead wiv that 1

Lewis
GRASSIC GIBBON

Real Name: John Leslie Mitchell, author of *A Scots Quair* and enjoyer of rural Aberdeenshire, 1901–1935

The land is pretty gr8, aint it

Aberdeenshire's the place 2 be

God's own country!!!

Yh yh its alrite

Yh ur rite

I h8 aberdeenshire

Full of hicks

nah it aint that bad

Ach ur rite

Finest place fur a man 2 live!!

. . . or is it?

what's better, cars or horses?

Uhhh I don't really know

They're pretty different

No they aren't

Cars are like machine horses

Which do you prefer?

Well they're both good in different ways . . .

Is this for your book?

Right

Exactly

I know what you're saying

Rocks are the best

Thanks!

SIR Henry
RAEBURN

You'd know his paintings if you saw one, 1756–1823

> Sup RaeRae, wot u been up2?

Oh u know, just painting an stuff

> Klkl, anything gd?

Nah nt rly

Got this weird one of a
reverend ice skating

> yh that is weird

stood on one leg for hours

on the ice!!!

> He must've rly wanted
> the painting done?

I dno like

Doesn't look like he's
having much fun

NNNOOOOOOOO

ahh what's up?!

I'VE RUN OUT OF BLACK PAINT

is that a total disaster?

. . .

WTF?!?!

YES

really? do many things need black paint?

yes! literally everything!

really? I'm just not seeing it

I dunno. you're the artist I guess

I just . . . like I'm looking around and I'm just seeing a lot of colour

well of course there's colour!

like sometimes there's red. or pale pink. maybe beige

but there's mainly black

everywhere

James
CHALMERS

The apparent inventor of the humble postage stamp, 1782–1853

Hey hows u?

I'm fine

But you know I hate this texting business

Y?

It's so impersonal

Its so quick tho!!

Gr8 for plannin a cheeky night out

Nope. I can't get on board with it

There's just no personal stamp

Whatcha dooooooin

Mehh just rolling around in paper

Rolling around in it?

Yeah. I just love paper

I got newspapers, stamps, envelopes, books

I just like paper man

You know what would be cool

If people could just send each other paper

You know, paper for all. That's just what I believe

Paper is pretty good I guess . . .

Zzup? ☺

Stop using those.

Using what? :O

Those!

"Emojis"

Why? :P

Because I'm boycotting them
until I get my royalties!

What? O.o

I invented small faces on
messages, OK!!?

OK ☺

Oh soz

Aaarrrgh!!!

;)

. . .

Kenneth GRAHAM

Author of the *Wind in the Willows*, which is a lovely book, 1859–1932

If u were a super rich toad

And needed to name
your giant mansion home

Wot would u call it?

> Emm . . .

> Ribbetlane Lodge?

> Toadworthington Estate?

> Hoppalong Hall Chateaux?

Hmmm

How about . . .

'Toad Hall'?

> . . . Sure

What about a super scary wood

It's really dark and creepy

What would you call that?

sigh

Frazzlebones Forest?

Grimblewood Grove?

Thornyclaw Thicket?

I like them

But

what do you think

Of Wild Wood :D

I hate you.

Y u stop being banker to write children's books??

It's very similar tbh.

Really??

Yea. You invent wild fictions that are complete fantasy, sell them to naïve people who don't know any better and get rich ;)

THE Mouse TO Robert BURNS

The unfortunate creature who had his family home destroyed by a madman wielding a plough. Poem romanticising his loss written in 1785.

> O wee mousie! The guilt I feel for recking ur home!
> U noble creature! U represent so much to me
> Our sad, sorry state of man
> Of all our future plans – w8ing to fall by the wayside!!

Rab

Hauld yer wheesht

But mousie... The poetry!!!!

Well u find the bairns a place 2 sleep then

See how poetic ur feelin then!

It's been weeks Rab, where's ma compensation?

O sweet mousie

I wrote you a poem!

It shall last through the ages!

Aye? An' wee Tammy's gonna rest her heid oan a poem at night eh?

I'll be waitin, Rab

Mousie I don't know what else to do??

Well then

Expect yir cheeses tae be nibbled.

John
STUART MILL

Wrote on utilitarian philosophy, liked to keep people happy, 1806–1873

John darling, would you like roast lamb for our dinner party on Saturday night?

Hey girl. Whatever makes everyone else happy is fine with me <3

But what's YOUR preference?

Honestly babe, whatever makes you all happy xoxo

John just give me a straight answer.

You know how much this annoys me.

I'm sorry honey 😠

Roast lamb sounds good. You're making me hungry! Nom nom xx

Too late.

Like, what would you say to curried fish tales in a spiced brussel sprout sauce? Would that be OK with you too?

You can't make me give up my life philosophies with curried fish tales, babe xxx

Fine.

But it would make everyone happier if you'd give up this nonsense

. . . Well now I'm just sad, hungry AND confused :'(

Allan
PINKERTON

A real baller. Founder of an American Detective Agency, saved the
President from an assassination plot, 1819–1884

I know what you did last summer

And this summer

. . . And maybe even next summer

Allan that's creepy

You're my friend but really you
have to stop 'practising' on me

Creepy? That's not what
the President said

He thinks I'm cool.

Also don't drink that milk,
look at the sell by date!

. . . I knew it

That IS you in the bushes

Me?!

Nope, I'm at home.

Actually I'm in the bath.

Definitely can't be me.

Allan I can see you trying to sneak away

Get off my flowerbeds!

I'm like the wind

Unseen, untraceable

I swear to God if you stand on one more pansy I will end you

Allan, is that you by the post office in a dress?

No Mr President, I surely do not know of what you speak

I am just a dainty lady

Waiting to post a letter to my sick mother

Allan, this is your phone number, I know it's you

We've spoken about this

I beg your pardon Mr President, I do believe you've got me mistaken for a rather daohing sounding fellow

But I am a lady. Posting letters

As you can see

Allan. Take a day off.

Andrew
CARNEGIE

Big name in the steel industry, big name in being rich, 1835–1919

I don't even like steel that much

Sure it makes me looooooads of money

But am I really happy??

Of course you're happy 'Drew

You could still be in Dumfermline you know

Being a weaver!

And you have a beautiful wife and daughter <3

But does money mean happiness, friend?

I just have sooooo much of it

I dunno what to do with it all!

I didn't actually mention money . . .

Honestly I get paid so much

You wouldn't even believe it

That's nice for you

And people keep offering me more

I'm practically sleeping on a bed of 100 dollah bills

OK you don't seem that sad.

Cash rules everything

James
BRAID

Made hypnosis science, apparently, 1795–1860

Hey girl

Hey . . . boy??

I've been staring at you all night ;)

Do you mean that as a compliment?

Yeah babe

OK cause it comes across as a little weird

Hey it's not my fault baby

It's yours for being so hot,
you got me hypnotised ;)

Sorry, hypno-what??

You know, when one is in a deep state of mental
concentration and focused so completely on a single
idea or train of thought that the Individual becomes
utterly unconscious of all other ideas, on goings or
impressions surrounding them

Ah, of course. How silly of me

. . . And this is your pick up technique??

Depends babe, is it working? ;)

. . . No. Goodbye.

James
CLERK MAXWELL

Did science and mathematics beyond a normal human's comprehension, 1831–1879

James, congrats on the publication!!!

Thanx bae, rly proud of myself #wellchuffed

Not going to lie though, I didn't really understand much of it

You're too smart!

Haha

Ur 2 kind x

Could you explain it to me? Maybe just the key ideas?

Jst stuff about electromagnetism x

And what does that mean? 😊

Eugh

I jst wrote a 500 word paper on it

Try Google

John
BUCHAN

Author of many things, liked Canada a lot, 1875–1940

> Darling there's a reporter at the house wanting to interview you xx

Ooooh exciting! Been a while since I've been interviewed!

Do you know what it's about?

> Think it's about The Thirty-Nine Steps xx

. . . 100 books

An ex-Conservative MP

A WAR correspondent. In REAL WARS.

I'm the goddamn Baron Tweedsmuir of Elsfield and the thirty fifth Governor General of Canada

. . . And all people ever ask about it The Thirty-Nine Steps!!!

> Well it was a rly gd book honey xx

We moved to Canada to escape this, Susan

> . . . I thought we moved for the new challenges and financial gains??

Sometimes I lie, Susan

Calgacus

Absolute hero and Defender Against the Romans, lived around 85AD

Chief, the Romans are coming!!

The who now?

The Romans!!! The lads in the shiny helmets an' that!

Big, pointy swords!

Ach away wi you!

Ain't nae man alive that kin take ma hame fi me!

Chief they're real pointy

Stabby stabby!

Ach fine, gather the lads an' we'll aff an' sort em out

Teach those cheeky foreigner lads a lesson!

. . .

Well sir that didnae go too well

An' nae yin's replying tae me!

. . . Chief???

THE Loch Ness MONSTER (NESSIE)

An aquatic enigma that, so far, eludes our friendship. Science would tell us she is perhaps 'not real', but dozens of stuffed animals created in her image tells us differently. Whether or not she wears a tartan cap in those murky waters of Loch Ness, or preserves her dignity and style with a more casual look, is another matter of contention. It is unknown how old the majestic Nessie is, or her true origins.

It'd be nice having someone to text

That's y u bot urself 2 phones

Yeah, but it's not the same, is it?

Well ur the 1 that decided 2 hang out @ the bottom of this lake

U chose this lyf

Be quiet, Nessie

Hey friend, how's things? xx

Sorry, who's this?

It's Nessie! You know, long, green gal who you've known like, FOREVER?? xx

Holy . . . What?! Nessie??? You're still alive?!

Yeah of course! Sorry it's been so long xx

Where have you been?!

Just wanted to take a break from the public eye xx

The photo shoots were getting stressful, not good for my anxiety xx

Aww Nessie, that sucks!

You can always talk to me about anything you know

Here for you fam'

Thanks Brad xx

Well, now you mention it

There's not much food left here

. . . So I've been nibbling on some tourists xx

Nessie! That's terrible! Are they OK?

Well no, cause I ate them :/ xx

NESSIE!!!!

And now the police are everywhere . . . They're gonna drain the loch 😞 xx

Nessie you can't just go round eating people.

Hi Kevin

Whose number is this?

It's the Loch Ness Monster

LOL

Nah, rly?

Really! I'm your new friend, Nessie

lol nessie doesn't have thumbs.
She wldnt be able to text!

Kevin, men have walked on the
moon. I've figured out how to
text without opposable thumbs

Yeah I guess so

omg

You're really Nessie then??

Yup

OMG

LOL

It's your Uncle Gavin

Got a new number

Robert THE Bruce's SPIDER

Although not a great weaver of webs, this little spider inspired the noble Robert the Bruce back to the bloody battlefields fighting against the English. He/she probably didn't live very long, being a spider, but he/she appears to have been living in his/her cave in roughly 1306.

Brucey boy yiv been in this cave fur months

Maybe you should git back oot there?

No Spider. My life is over.

This cave is my home now.

Laddie dinnae give me that nonconse

Everything is meaningless.

The English have won and my life is worthless.

Sonny quit talking like that

And dinnae make me gie you a pep talk

I've got my hardships too ya ken

Oh Spidey

What could you know of the hardships of man?

Dinnae be so dramatic Brucey boy

I cannae keep up these wee counselling sessions much longer

My web's taking furever tae build!

A mere web, good friend.

But wait . . .

What if that web were a metaphor?

And your staunch tenacity a message from our good Lord?!

Aye whatever you say Brucey boy

I really got tae get on though

Them flies dinnae catch themselves

The Haggis IN REPLY TO 'ADDRESS TO A HAGGIS'

Written in 1786, Robert Burns terrorised the haggis community with this brutal, cannibalistic poem.

I appreciate all the niceties, friend

Does this mean you'll let me go free?

It's time tae cut ye up wi' ready sleight!

That doesn't really sound like something I'd be into . . .

Haggis!

Trenching your gushing entrails bright, like onie ditch;

What a glorious sight!

Well I do say, that sounds rather barbaric actually . . .

Horn for horn, they stretch an' strive!

Oh come on, you're making this so much worse

Deil tak the hindmost!

I'm sorry, what??

But mark the Rustic, haggis-fed

The trembling earth resounds his tread!

That's it then; the end is nigh

To be consumed by a madman

Give Scotland her Haggis!!!!

Saint
MUNGO

Patron Saint of Glasgow and enjoyer of working a cheeky miracle, 528–614

Being a Saint isn't all fun and games you know

Aye, sure

Sitting in yir monastery, probably oan the Buckfast

What a terrible life

Don't be disrespectful to the Lord's work, friend

Miracles take much rest and energy to perform

And much Bucky, eh pal?

Hahaha

Well, it is Glasgow tbf

One has to fit in with the locals ;)

Black AGNES

Righteously and boldly defended Dunbar Castle against a ferocious English siege. Refused to give up and eventually the English abandoned their wicked schemes. However, 'Black Agnes' is still named after her image. Come on, guys who wrote history. 1312–1369

Hey giiiiirl, haven't seen u in ages! Hows u?

OMG Stephaniiiie! Hi hi hi! I know it's been 4ever!

I'm OK yeah, a bit busy atm. U?

Oh you know, the usual ☺ Wot u been up2?

Well . . . Hubby went away with the army a while ago

I've kinda been under siege for a few months :/

. . . omg, wot??

Yh this guy wants my castle but I'm like NAH!

Hahahaha omg ur so funnieh

So proud of u girl <3

Thanx Stephanie xoxo

We have ur Brother

Sorry, who is this?

It's the English

Oh cool

How is John, then?

He's fine, but we're going to hang him if u don't surrender.

4 real??

4 real.

Damn . . .

You'd better get the noose out then #lol

Excuse me?!

Well . . . I'll get all his stuff, won't I?

Idiots

ffs Agnes, plz just give up ur making us look bad

#winning #siegegirl #dontstopmenow

Thomas
CARLYLE

Wrote many interesting things across the board, 1795–1881

Do u think if I write about famous dudes enough I'll become one?

Emm, not sure if that's how it works pal

I'm gonna do it anyway

Great, Thomas, you go and do that

I'm gonna write a whole book about the dudes I love

Or maybe just WHY dudes are so great

klkl

Bros lovin' bros

You know what Harry

What mate?

'University experience' my arse.

I'm traumatised

God is not real

What is real

I know nothing

Who am I?

KING William THE Lion

Fought the English a lot, 1143–1214

That was a wee bitty embarrassing!

Sir, ye charged the English army . . . By yirself

Aye, but how wis I tae ken I'd lose?!

Well sir, ye were vastly oot numbered

Being only yin man an' aw . . .

True, true . . . Aye well, wit can ye do eh

Sir ye lost oor independence!

Ach we'll git it back

Just leave it wi me

I am king!

Yes we know.

I shall have a flag that represents me and it shall bear a fierce animal!

A bear?

No, bear!

As in carry.

You're going to carry a bear?

No!

I want to have an animal on my flag.

How is anyone going to see your flag if an animal is lying on it?

No you eejit!

There shall be an animal sewn into the fabric of my flag.

That's just cruel . . .

Anyway, it would have to be tiny or else it would tear.

. . .

I want to have the image of a fierce animal, which represents me, embroidered onto the flag!!!

Understand???

Oh I see . . .

Thank God!

Which animal?

A fox?

Ginger cat, perhaps?

A lion!

Really?

. . .

Just make the stupid flag already!

SCOTLAND THE TEXT

Michael
SCOTT

A real Scottish wizard. (Honestly! look him up.) Died in 1236(ish)

I try my best to educate myself, and what do I get back?

You tell me Michael

You're the wizard round here

EXACTLY

Oxford educated, further studies in Paris, translated some of the world's finest philosophy!!

And this is what I get. Big bushy beard and pointy hat chat

Awright Merlin, calm down

I WILL NOT CALM DOWN

I don't have much longer to live see

What?? Are you ill?? 😟 </3

Nah, but a small pebble will fall on my head and I will die

. . . And how do you know that?

The stars told me

Yir a wizard, Michael

You have to fire Jim!

Who are you?

It's me, Dwight.

...

Stop confusing me with your boss!

Oh I see . . .

Are we playing a game to confuse Jim?

OMG!

Get back to *The Office*!

James
HOGG

A man of letters, literary pals with Walter Scott, 1770–1835

Hey Walter, got a novel idea

Aye?

It's gonna be wild

Could be read as a supernatural thriller . . .

OR as a study of the psychology behind religious fanaticism

Hmmm

I don't know, sounds a bit much?

I'm just getting started!

Playing with one story . . . But from two perspectives!!

Look, James, I'll be real with you

That sounds a bit rubbish

. . . You're joking??

Yeah man, sorry

Maybe try something a bit more . . . Historical?

Oh like the Jacobite Rebellion was so much fun

James.

Yes, darling wife

What's this I hear about you moving on from The Three Perils of Man to some other piece of codswallop

Yeah, I've got a great new idea

How very dare you

I don't know what I've done wrong . . .

I suppose women have no perils, hmm?

I'm here dropping baby girls for you but no, nothing perilous about being a woman

That's not what I meant!

And you can take 'man' as universal?

Babe?

You're a real selfish asshole

Don't be like this!

Might find something very perilous indeed in your dinner tonight.

OK ok I'll write one about women too

Men.

William
PATERSON

The Scottish chap who founded the Bank of England, 1658–1719

Goddamn I'm gonna be SO RICH

. . . w/e Willy

It might not work out u know

PSSSSHHHHT

m8 I'm setting up a damn BANK

Gonna be rollin' in dough

Well we'll wait and c

CASH CASH MONEY

hey pal, hows u?

I'm gd willie. u? wubu2?

I'm ok . . . Got kicked out the bank

Sorry to hear that man (also: WHAAAAAY)

But I refuse to be kept down!

Oh god . . .

So England has a bank now . . .

Here we go . . .

Time for Scotland

Bring it, bitches.

Bring in dem dollah bills

. . . Sterling, man, sterling.

Yeah, but Sterling notes don't have the same ring to it

'rollin in them sterling notes'

Bit rubbish, eh?

Hmmmm

Yeah I see what you mean

KING David I

Another fighter of the English – as was popular in them days, 1124–1153

Sup Matilda

Oh hey uncle, what's up?

Nothin much. Chilling in the North

cool cool

Was wondering if u wanted help getting the ol' English throne?

Ooooh uncle, that'd be awesome!

One condition, though.

. . . Depends what it is?

I get Newcastle.

Emm . . . Sure? Why?

Banter, my dear. Banter.

Elsie
INGLIS

The Victorian #bossbitch who founded the Scottish Women's Suffragette Federation, 1864–1917

> Sorry babe women just cant study medicine xx

Pah

You can't hold me down

> Babe just come over? xx

> You can make me that casserole I love so much xx

Make your own goddamn casserole

I'm busy saving lives

LADY LIVES

THE Chap WHO INVENTED Golf

In 1744 some smart guy finally had the bright idea of writing down the rules to a game the Scots had been playing for centuries. Thankfully the writing down took place in Edinburgh, so credit's still due to this noble nation of rolling fields and fake sand pits.

Hey man, wanna grab a few beers this afternoon?

Maybe try out this new game I thought of?

Sure thing man, what's the game?

Well

Get this

You have a wee hole in the grass

Get a club

and whack a wee ball into the hole from really far away

. . . Ok

Is that it?

And we do this like, 18 times

Nah there's a bunch of rules and stuff

But we can get to that later ☺

Sorry Colin

Turns out I'm busy

Oh, ok ☹

Doing what?

Literally anything else

Man it's so boring here in the countryside . . .

There's stuff we can do!

Yea?

Do you want to go to play hockey?

Too much running . . .

Go for a drive?

Dunno, we only have the beach buggy atm . . .

Or just stay home in pajamas and do nothing?

No, we need to do *something*!

Wait . . .

I've just had a brilliant idea!

??

THE Mad Men THAT INVENTED Curling

Picture it: it's winter 1540, and you're bored oot yir nut. You're a John Sclater, a monk at Paisley Abbey, and there's a dazzling frozen lake near your abbey. You challenge your buddy Gav, a pal of the abbot, to a game of sliding stones over the ice and seeing what mad banter goes down.

Cheers for coming out the day Gav

Nae worries man, good game

Aye my stanes went SO FAR

Aye but mines went faster

w/e Gav, speed isnae wot matters

Aye but they had precision tae

My aim was exact and true

. . . Gav go an' no go on eh man

We hud banter, that's wot counts

True

It's no even a real game

YOU TAKE THAT BACK SIR

ADMIRAL Thomas COCHRANE

Named the Sea Wolf by Napoleon himself; an undeniably cool nickname of which all should be envious, 1775–1860

> So what, are you an admiral or an Earl or wot?

I am everything

> Aye but like, which yin?

Jock I am the wind in the sails of Britain's finest ships

I am the great waves which carry us unto Victory

> Aye aye, but I just wanna know wot to call you?

The very spirit of naval Britannia – I AM SHE.

> You're a she, sir?

No I am speaking in metaphors, pleb

Justice hath no name

SIR James
Y SIMPSON

Not the actual inventor of chloroform, but the main man that made it popular in medicine. (Which kinda counts, right?) 1811–1870

Fancy helping a brother out?

Sure thing

What do I have to do?

Oh, just go to sleep for a little while . . .

Is that it??

Yup

. . . ☺

Robert
STEVENSON

An engineer who designed and built lighthouses, 1772–1850. Not to be confused with Robert Louis Stevenson . . .

Hey, is this Robert Stevenson?

Yes?

Love your work!

Oh, thank you!

Are you a sailor?

Sailor? No.

But I adored Treasure Island!

Treasure Island? I don't think I've worked there . . .

Do you mean Bell Rock?

Bell Rock? Is that a new one!??

Fairly . . .

Where's it set?

In Orkney.

Haven't read that one.

Read?

Yea I've only read *Treasure Island* and *The Strange Case of Dr. Jekyll and Mr. Hyde*.

. . .

I AM NOT ROBERT LOUIS STEVENSON!!!

James
MACPHERSON

A renowned poet and gifted 'translator' (also to be understood as 'trickster' or 'bender of truth'), 1736–1796.

omg just read Fingal

amazing

oh really? yeah it's good huh

so, you just found it?

uhh. yeah pretty much.

where?

hmm?

where did you find it?

oh. uh it was just sort of lying there

under a rock

beside

some trees

wow. and it's a lost Gaelic epic or something?

yeah that's about right.

and you translated it into the English language? this ancient transcript of prehistoric folklore? never before seen or heard of? bringing you massive fame and fortune?

YES ok enough with the fifth degree I definitely did all of these things

George BROWN

Got tired of Scotland, decided to invent Canada, 1818–1880.

Man it's so cold in Scotland ☹

Then why don't you move?

I will!

Where?

My friend in America said there's this huge bit of land that no one has claimed yet. Very warm, apparently; right next to a place called "Greenland".

I'll go there and start my own country!

...

??

Nothing, George . . .

Inspector
REBUS

Fictional detective who guides the reader around the "real" Edinburgh.
Also drinks a lot.

I want to show people the
true side of Edinburgh!

Who are you?

I'm Inspector Rebus!

I show people the dark
side of this city.

It's always dark.

I show Edinburgh's true nature!

You mean the parks?

No!

The dark human nature of the city!

Oh.

Like Robert Louis Stevenson did?

No!

The modern Edinburgh!

Like in *Trainspotting*?

I was here first! Why does Irvine
Welsh get all the credit?!